MODELING JESUS: WALKING SINGLEMINDED IN A DOUBLEMINDED WORLD
Study Guide

Throughout this study, we will explore, as a group and individually, what it means to "walk single-minded" and how this concept is pivotal in helping ourselves, and others to navigate this world in the light that our Father has provided for us. We will go in-depth through the insight found in **MODELING JESUS: WALKING SINGLEMINDED IN DOUBLEMINDED WORLD** by Brad Climer. This is an opportunity to do more than just read another Christian self-help book. This is a tool to help us dig deep into understanding an amazing life-changing revelation and help us make it our own.

Interior formatting by Hannah Linder Designs

Instructions for using this study guide

Each session contains various components: pre-session questions, session reading, scripture references, discussion questions, author's favorite quote, session take away, and suggested prayer generated by each session's theme.

The **pre-session questions** are designed to be answered before the participants have done any reading for that session. They can be used as homework during the week in preparation for the next week's session and used at the beginning of the session as an opening discussion.

The **session reading** can be shared aloud by the participants, or the audible version can be accessed during class. The author himself reads the audible book, and using this version gives the feel of having the session material taught by Pastor Brad.

Scriptures used throughout the chapter reading are listed in each section of the study guide for ease in looking them up for further study. The author hopes that each participant will desire to look further into God's word and desire to hear Him more clearly on each theme.

The **discussion questions** are designed to help the participants not only dig deeper into understanding the theme of each session but also open dialogue in the group setting, which will allow for further development of understanding as each person's view will help add insight into what is being taught.

The author has included in each session his **favorite quote** from that chapter. These are points of particular importance for further meditation and discussion. This quote can be used to lead into the session takeaway discussion.

Session takeaway is the opportunity for each participant to share with the group what in particular stands out as most important to them. In teaching at Pastor Brad's ministry, he often uses this technique to hear what people are grasping out of his messages. In the group study setting, this often brings out some unique "aha" moments.

Finally, there are suggested **prayer points** for taking the theme to our Father and sealing in prayer what has been received during the session. Some sessions include a crafted prayer and others only points with which the participants may create their prayers. This should be encouraged by the session leader.

Each session is designed to be approximately 90 minutes in length. The group leader is integral in facilitating the flow of the session and allowing each participant to have a voice in the discussions. Discussion questions can also be used in larger groups as breakout sessions, and a breakout leader can give a report of the discussion when the groups are called back to the large group setting.

Desired outcomes for this study

1. Fall in love with our Father
2. Honor and follow Him
3. Put His opinion above every other
4. Prefer others above ourselves
5. Improve our love walk
6. Be about Father's business

Session 1

In this opening session, participants should introduce themselves and briefly explain why they are attending this study. Since this is the first session, the group leader should use the pre-session questions to generate an understanding and direction for further lessons and the overall theme of this study. It is suggested that after this opening session, each participant prepares the pre-session questions during the week as homework and comes to the session prepared to discuss their answers at the beginning of each session.

Presession Questions:

1. What comes to mind when you read the title "Modeling Jesus?"

2. What do the terms "single-minded" and "double-minded" mean to you?

3. What do you currently think "walking single-minded in a double-minded world" means?

Read: Preface (4.55 minutes) (audio 00:23-5:18)

Scripture references:
Ephesians 4:11-13

Discussion questions:

1. Explore a time when you felt like you had experienced "defeat in your Christian walk."

____
____
____
____
____
____
____

2. To which feeling that the author expressed, do you most relate and why?

____
____
____
____
____
____
____

3. What is the spirit of religion? What are the five gifts the spirit of religion has left the earth?

____
____
____
____
____
____
____

4. Compare and contrast the five-fold ministry (Eph 4:11-13) with the five "gifts" of the spirit of religion?

5. How have you been affected by the five "gifts" of the spirit of religion?

Author's Favorite Quote:
"My friend said to me, 'What you miss is the time with your Father."

Session take-away:

Before we go further into this study, let's stop for a minute and consider this quote. Do you know that you have a loving Father? Have you been spending time with your Father? Let's take a minute here to understand where each participant is concerning their relationship with God. Do all have a personal relationship with God? Share further what you feel you have gained from this session.

PRAYER:

Father,

I pray for a relationship with You that is holy, pure, and true. I desire to spend more intimate time with you and my heart is open and receptive to Your word. I pray as I gather together with my brothers and sisters seeking You, that we grow together in our love for You and each other. I am excited to begin this journey together. Lord, hold our hands as we tread this path of revelation together. Help us to be free of religion and to grow in our relationship. Teach us what it means to be "single-minded."

In Jesus' name,
Amen.

Session 2

In this session, we will be introduced to the concept that Jesus modeled a life of following His Father in every life situation. Because He walked on this earth as a human being, He is the example for us in everything. By observing how Jesus walked in this world, we can see how we too are able to walk as Jesus walked. He models for us how to stay "single-minded."

Presession questions:

1. What is your current idea of a "perfect" life? What is your view of success?

2. Which areas of your life seem more prone to drama than others and what are you currently doing about them?

3. How do you think Jesus got through life situations? How do you support your view?

Read: Introduction (4:15 minutes) (audio 5:23-9:38)

Scripture references:

Luke 19:10; 1 John 4:17; Hebrews 12:1; Romans 14:23; Revelation 2:4; Matthew 5:14

Discussion questions:

1. Jesus is our model in everything. What do you think Jesus considered a success and "perfect" life? What kept Jesus able to stay out of drama?

2. What was Jesus' purpose on earth? Discuss Luke 19:10. How does knowing your purpose help you to stay out of drama? Discuss how the loss of focus might be what is spoken of in Hebrews 12:1.

3. What does 1 John 4:17 “as He is, so are We in This world,” mean to you? How does this connect with Matthew 5:14?

4. In what areas of your life do you currently feel you are struggling to know how God wants you to handle them? What does "anything not of faith is sin" (Romans 14:23) mean to you?

____
____
____
____
____
____
____

5. How do we let Holy Spirit lead us as He did Jesus? How might Revelation 2:4 apply here?

____
____
____
____
____
____
____

Author's Favorite Quote:

"There is no life situation we will face that Jesus hasn't already experienced -- not only experienced but overcome. That makes the concept of being single-minded, like He was, so important for us."

Session take-away:

As we wrap up this second session, think about all the different situations you find yourself facing in life. How do those situations compare to the ones that Jesus experienced? In what ways can you see the example of Jesus bringing light into how you might handle your situations? What would it mean to you to be single-minded about those situations? Share further what you feel you have gained from this session.

____
____
____
____
____

Prayer:

Father,

As we explore what success means in our lives, let us reflect on how Jesus demonstrated your perfect will. Dear Lord, let us look to You for heavenly riches and not earthly pleasures. Let us consider what you have purposed for us in Spirit and in truth. Let us remember how Jesus stayed focused on Your instructions. Help us to be prepared to follow your voice in all we endeavor.

In Jesus' name,
Amen.

Session 3

In session 3, we will explore Mark 4:13 and learn how it can become a *true* reality in our lives and open up the scriptures in a dynamic way. Pastor Brad found this to be a pivotal statement and he shares this fresh perspective with his readers.

Presession questions:

1. Would you describe yourself as open-minded or hard-headed and why?

____
____
____
____
____
____
____

2. Would you describe yourself as a "black & white" person or do you see that there are some "gray" areas?

____
____
____
____
____
____
____

3. How clearly do you feel you understand Scripture?

____
____
____
____
____
____
____

4. Describe a topic that you were "sure" you understood and then the experience of "changing your mind." How did that feel? Describe.

Read: Single- vs Double-mindedness (ch1)

(pg 1-4)(6:40 minutes)(audio 9:39-16:19)

Scripture references:

Mark 4:13; Philippians 3:14; Isaiah 50:7; John 14:12; 1 Corinthians 11:1; Deuteronomy 31:6; 1 John 5:4

Discussion questions:

1. What is Jesus saying to His disciples in Mark 4:13? To what is He referring?

2. How can we finally make Mark 4:13 a *true* reality in our life?

3. Define "mystery." Based on your definition, discuss how you pursue growth in your understanding of God's word.

4. Looking at the context of Isaiah 50:7, what does it mean to have your "face set like flint" and in what ways/areas of your life might you need to do this so you can grow in God?

5. What was the single-minded perspective of Jesus in John 14:12 and Paul in 1 Corinthians 11:1? Given these examples, what should our perspective be?

AUTHOR'S FAVORITE QUOTE

"If we don't understand what Scripture is saying, we can be double-minded to His will and instructions."

SESSION TAKE-AWAY:

Looking at this quote from the author, how important is our growth in our understanding of scripture? How much effect will our understanding have on our ability to walk single-minded in a double-minded world? Share further what you feel you have gained from this session.

PRAYER:

Father,

Thank you for Your living word that saves us. Your word is hope, truth, and freedom. Holy Spirit helps us to sow seeds in will with Father. Let His truth and love spread and grow. Help us not to hesitate in dropping our seeds urgently and earnestly in love.

In Jesus' name,
Amen.

SESSION 4

Session 4 begins our two-part study of the parable often entitled the Parable of the Sower. We shall see within session 4 and session 5 that this parable would be more aptly titled the Parable of the Soils for the concentration is not on the Sower as much as it is on the soil types. We shall see in these next two sessions why Jesus emphasized the importance of understanding this parable and why it is key to understanding the rest of scripture. This understanding is essential to "walking single-minded in a double-minded world."

PRESESSION QUESTIONS:

1. What is a parable and how did Jesus use them as He taught?

2. How familiar are you with "the Parable of The Sower?" Discuss your current understanding of this parable.

3. For what reasons do you think Jesus would point to this parable as being a pivotal passage based on the discussion of Chapter 1 in our last session?

Read: The Parable of the Sower (ch2) (part 1) (pg 5-11)
(12:39 minutes) (audio16:20-28:59)

Scripture references:
Mark 4:3-20; 1 Peter 2:24; John 10:27; Proverbs 13:12; Proverbs 17:9; Philippians 4:19; James 1:23; John 5:19; John 8:28

Discussion questions:

1. What are some other terms for "seed" that one might use to help explain the concept found here?

2. Demonstrate how one might use this concept to begin a "single-minded" approach to a problem.

3. To what does the "soil" refer? Discuss the three types of soil we have read about so far. How do you see this applying to you?

4. How do we identify our current soil type?

5. What do you think is Jesus' soil type? How do we become like Jesus' "soil type?"

Author's favorite quote:

"Jesus expressed it as being a pivotal revelation. Understanding this opened a fresh understanding of the entire Bible for me, and I want to share it with you."

Session take-away:

As we end part one of the two-part study on this parable, discuss the author's favorite quote from this section. What is the "it" that Jesus considered pivotal revelation? How does this understanding open up a fresh understanding of Scripture? What have you learned so far about this parable and how can this be applied to your life?

Prayer:

Father,

I pray that you till the ground in my life, that it may not be hardened, stoney, or thorny. Cause it to be the good soil that receives the word. May that word grow and bring forth a hundredfold harvest in my life.

In Jesus' name,
Amen.

Session 5

This session picks up as the author continues his look at the parable contained in Mark 4:1-20 as Jesus is expounding on the "good seed." Jesus modeled for us a place where we can learn to walk. We can learn to walk in the place of one hundred percent.

Presession questions:

1. Recap the first section of this chapter. Discuss the seed and the three soil types studied in the last session.

2. What will be your first steps to improve your "soil" based on the soil type you identified in the previous session?

3. Do you think we are able to become like Jesus' "soil type?" How?

Read: The Parable of the Sower (ch 2) (part 2) (pg 11-14)
(7:30 minutes) (audio 29:00-36:30)

Scripture references:
Mark 4:3-20; 1 Peter 2:24; John 10:27; Proverbs 13:12; Proverbs 17:9; Philippians 4:19; James 1:23; John 5:19; John 8:28

Discussion questions:

1. Compare and contrast the three soil types from the last session with the "good" soil we read about in this session.

____
____
____
____
____
____
____

2. Do you think what Jesus spoke of in John 5:19 and John 8:28 might be keys to "walking single-minded in a double-minded world?" How would you apply them to your life?

____
____
____
____
____
____
____

3. Discuss the birds. Are you able to identify where they land and pick off seeds in your life? What will you do differently based on this understanding?

____
____
____
____
____
____
____

4. What does the word "hearing" mean to you? Is it possible to hear and yet not really "hear?" Elaborate on a time when this might have happened to you.

5. Does acting in obedience in response to what you hear make the difference between hearing and "hearing?" Discuss what you think about this concept. How might you apply it to your life?

Author's favorite quote:

"One hundred percent is the realm Jesus walked in and He intends us to walk in."

Session take-away:

In this session, we finished looking at the parable that Jesus said was the most pivotal for understanding everything else in Scripture. Pivotal in our ability for "walking single-minded in a double-minded world." Discuss the author's favorite quote above. How did Jesus walk "one hundred percent?" Remember since Jesus modeled it, we can walk in it as well. We can change the soil in our life. We can all go to good soil. What are some things that we should do to be in the process of improving our soil? What else have you learned in this session?

Prayer:

Father,

I want my soil type, my mindset and my attitudes, to be like Jesus' soil. Teach me how to be single-minded to Your instructions. Teach me how to let You till my soil so I can produce one hundredfold as Jesus did. Show me that this can be the reality in my life. Show me how to cooperate with You in this process.

In Jesus' name,
Amen.

Session 6

In this session, we will begin an exploration of chapter 3 in "Modeling Jesus: Walking Single-minded in a Double-minded World." This chapter will be covered in four sessions as we see that the concept of single-mindedness can be found in "All Through The Bible." One can discover this concept in the Garden of Eden. This session will look at the single-minded instruction of God as well as Adam and Eve's double-minded response and what havoc that response produced.

Presession questions:

1. Based on the last two sessions, which soil type produces a harvest, and what do you think are some ways to increase that harvest?

2. How do the concepts of single-minded and double-minded relate to the soil types and harvest?

3. Discuss your current understanding of Adam and Eve.

Read: All Through the Bible (ch 3) (Part 1 Adam and Eve)

(pg 15-18)
(7:16 minutes)(audio 36:31-43:47)

Scripture references:
Genesis 2:15-17; Genesis 3:5-6; Ezekiel 28; Isaiah 14

Discussion questions:

1. What was the single-minded instruction of God to Adam and Eve? What was their double-minded response?

2. How does disobedience to Father's instructions cause separation in our fellowship with God?

3. What is a "situational atheist?" Have you ever done this? How?

4. Explain the difference between earthly and Godly wisdom.

5.Wh at are some ways that we make the choice to not hear our Heavenly Father daily?

Author's favorite quote:

"Being double-minded is always costly. When we break fellowship with the Father, we start fellowshipping with something else. The 'something else' could be care, concern, or our human reasoning, or it could be circumstance thrown at us in this natural life."

Session take-away:

Adam and Eve, unfortunately, modeled that their wandering eye leads them from the instructions Father had delivered for them. They have now considered an alternative to being in God's will. Have we done that as well? What areas do we need to consider so we can get back into fellowship with our Father? What else have you received from this fresh look at Adam and Eve from the perspective of single vs double-minded?

PRAYER:

Father,

You show me in Your Word that I can be single-minded and the consequences of being double-minded. Help me to see the difference between hearing Your instructions and being led astray by the voice of the enemy. Help me to hear You daily and to not consider Your instructions to be optional. Help me to understand the difference between earthly and heavenly wisdom and to desire to follow You in every area of my life.

In Jesus' name,
Amen.

SESSION 7

In this session, we will begin a two-part exploration of the account of David and his encounter with Goliath. The author states, "this is one of the best examples of being single-minded in the Bible." While to many this is just a cute story that we heard in Sunday school, during the next two sessions we will discover how David's single-minded focus helped him to overcome what seemed to everyone else a hopeless situation with insurmountable odds. Read 1 Samuel 17 to refresh your recollection of David's story.

PRESESSION QUESTIONS:

1. What are some seemingly hopeless and insurmountable situations that you are currently facing in your life?

2. Do you think fear plays into the decisions you make in life? Discuss a time when you did or didn't do something because of fear?

3. What effect do you see that fear plays on your ability to stay single-minded to Father's instructions?

Read: All Through the Bible (ch 3) (Part 2 David and Goliath) (pg 18-23) (7:58 min)(audio 43:48-51:46)

Scripture references:
1 Samuel 17; Psalm 46:1

Discussion questions:

1. The Philistines were trespassing on Judah's land. What can this be compared to in our lives today?

2. Goliath was a loud-mouth and intimidating individual. He obviously was overwhelming to Judah. Are you overcome by Goliath's in your life to the point that you are double-minded by obvious disadvantages? In what areas do you see this occurring?

3. Israel was dismayed and greatly afraid because of Goliath. Discuss a time when you were dismayed and greatly afraid. How did you get through this time?

4. Why was David so different from the rest of Israel? What did he know that the rest of the nation didn't?

5. How can we be as single-minded to Heavenly instruction as David was?

Author's favorite quote:

"This story is one of the best examples of being single-minded in the Bible."

"The Enemy also wants us to fall into drama (conflict)."

Session take-away:

For what purpose does the enemy try to get us into drama? How do we see David avoid drama and be about his Father's business? What have you learned from this first part of David's story and how will you apply it this week?

Prayer:

Father,

Thank you for bringing me into an awareness that drama is the enemy trespassing in my life and attempting to distract me from a single-minded focus on Your instructions for my life. Help me to keep my eyes and ears tuned in to what You are doing instead of being distracted by the taunting and intimidation of the enemy. I refuse to be dismayed or afraid. I focus on You.

In Jesus' name,
Amen.

Session 8

This session finishes the section on David and Goliath by exploring the concept of authenticity and "killing" a problem through the use of the weapons given us in our instructions from God.

Presession questions:

1.Wha t have you gained about being single-minded from the first session on David and Goliath?

____
____
____
____
____
____
____

2. Have you identified any trespassers on your land and how have you dealt with them differently this week?

____
____
____
____
____
____
____

3. Have you asked, "How am I seen in heaven?" What have you heard for an answer?" Name two ways that you are seen in heaven.

____
____
____
____
____
____
____

Read: All Through the Bible (ch 3) (Part 3 David and Goliath cont.) (pg 23-27)(11:26 min)(audio 51:46-103:12)

Scripture references:
1 Samuel 17; Hebrews 13:5; Ephesians 5:26; Romans 8:37; Genesis 50:20; Exodus 20:3

Discussion questions:

1. David was not motivated to take on Goliath by the reward offered by Saul. He was motivated by the fact that Goliath was coming against God's honor. What is currently motivating you to seek God? Do your problems or desiring an answer to some situation motivate you more than the desire to be with your Father? Do you desire to be about your Father's business, or do you prefer that Father be about your business?

2. David picked up five smooth stones out of the brook. Goliath had brothers, but David was ready for them. What are five Philistine giants in your life? What are five smooth stones from the Holy Spirit with which you can slay them?

3. David ran at Goliath. Why do you think he was able to do that? Do you run at your problems or from them? Explain.

4. David did not see himself as inadequate to the task of killing Goliath even though he did not have a sword. What inadequacies do you see in yourself that, focusing on them, will cause you to see yourself as limited instead of "able to do all things through Christ who strengthens you?"

____
____
____
____
____
____
____

5. Goliath tries to impose his will upon David. David says, "No!" and beheads him. Goliath represents problems in our lives that attempt to be head over us when Christ is head. How can you apply this in your life? What issues do you face that are trying to be your head? How can you behead that problem and have Christ back in the position of the head?

____
____
____
____
____
____
____

Author's favorite quote:

"David's decision to be authentic and not wear Saul's armor which he had never worn before, was what kept him safe. He could now operate in his true self."

Session take-away:

No armor. Only his authentic self. Many times even when we speak God's word if it doesn't really mean anything to us, it is only like wearing Saul's armor. To wear Saul's armor may represent trying to walk in someone else's faith, trying to walk in another's anointing or speaking scripture without really having any understanding of it. Is it possible to learn to be authentic like David was? What else have you gained from this study of David and Goliath?

____
____

Prayer:

Father,

Teach me how to pick up smooth stones from Your word. Teach me to put on only who You say I am and to be authentic to myself. Speak to me and give me instructions from Your word and help me to keep Your word alive in me.

In Jesus' name,
Amen.

SESSION 9

This last session in chapter 3. "All Through the Bible" will explore the single-minded focus found in some of the people included in Hebrews 11. This passage of scripture is often entitled the Hall of Faith.

PRESESSION QUESTIONS:

1. Consider that the purpose of the stories or testimonies of how other people have learned to "walk in faith" or "walk single-minded" is to encourage us to walk closer to the Lord. Do you feel encouraged or like you don't measure up? What do you think is happening to you when you feel "less than" someone else?

____

____

____

____

____

____

____

2. Read Hebrews 12:1-3 from the Message Bible: "Do you see what this means—all these pioneers who blazed the way, all these veterans cheering us on? It means we'd better get on with it. Strip down, start running—and never quit! No extra spiritual fat, no parasitic sins. Keep your eyes on *Jesus*, who both began and finished this race we're in. Study how he did it. Because he never lost sight of where he was headed—that exhilarating finish in and with God—he could put up with anything along the way: Cross, shame, whatever. And now he's *there*, in the place of honor, right alongside God. When you find yourselves flagging in your faith, go over that story again, item by item, that long litany of hostility he plowed through. *That* will shoot adrenaline into your souls!" Discuss this scripture and how it pertains to "walking single-minded in a double-minded world.

____

____

____

____

____

____

____

3. What kind of an example are you to those around you? In what areas are you encouraging and what areas need improvement?

____

____

Read: All Through the Bible(ch 3) (Part 4 Hall of Faith) (pg 27-30)
(5:30 min)(audio 1:03-1:08:42)

Scripture references:
Hebrews 11: 7, 29-30

Discussion questions:

1. Noah is an example of "walking single-minded in a double-minded world." By following the instructions he had from Father, he looked insane to those around him. He had to believe in the midst of unbelief. How does following Father's instructions in your life affect the way others see you? Do you have friends or family that think you are "crazy" for believing? How do you deal with this in your life?

2. Moses is an example of "walking single-minded in a double-minded world." He had to be single-minded to Father's instructions as the leader of the double-minded people that he led. How difficult is it to lead people, with a single-minded focus on Father's instructions, when double-minded suggestions and opinions bombard the leaders? How as a leader, parent, employer, etc. do you stay single-minded?

3. The Israelites throughout their recorded history are examples of walking both double-minded and single-minded. In the wilderness experience, they often murmured and complained and gave their leaders a difficult time. Imagine how difficult it must have been to keep the whole Israelite army single-minded about their instructions to besiege Jericho. What are some of the difficulties that present themselves when trying to stay single-minded as an individual? How are these magnified when trying to lead a double-minded group?

4. The author states that instability comes when two opposing forces enter our thinking. What examples do you find in your own life of two opposing thoughts which cause instability?

5. Sessions 6-9 have looked at examples of single-minded and double-minded as they are found "All Through the Bible." What are other examples that have not been covered and what lessons do you see in that example?

Author's favorite quote:

"God has put everything in us that we need to be faith beings. Holy Spirit is there, living inside us, and He is enforcing what was put in us. We are overcomers in this life."

Session take-away:

2 Peter 1:3 tells us that God has given us everything that pertains to life and godliness. What is left out of "everything?" How do we learn to access what Father has put in us? How do we stop wavering and being unstable? What else did you receive from this session?

____

____

____

____

____

____

____

Prayer:

Father,

You have created me to be a faith being. According to Your word, those that have gone before me are cheering me on as I run my race. Help me to follow their examples of faith. Your word also says that You have given me everything that I need to live this life for You. Help me to follow Your instructions, to access You, and be stable and unwavering.

In Jesus' name,
Amen.

Session 10

This session begins a two-part exploration of the concept of good versus evil. Do images of a good person with a halo over their head and another person with a pitchfork and a tail come to mind? Or perhaps the good person is the granny in a rocking chair and the evil one a burly dude in leather and chains? These caricatures of good and evil do not present the real nature of either good or evil. In this session, the author will look again at Adam and Eve and what good versus evil means in the context of "walking single-minded in a double-minded world."

Presession questions:

1. How would you currently define "good" and "evil?"

____
____
____
____
____
____
____

2. In what way do you think Hollywood dramatizations play into the views of "good versus evil" today? How does it affect your thinking on this subject?

____
____
____
____
____
____
____

3. Read Romans 16:19. What does it mean to be "wise in what is good, and innocent in what is evil?"

____
____
____
____
____

Read: Good vs Evil (ch 4) part 1 (pg 31-34)
(7:27 min)(audio 1:08:42-1:16:09)

Scripture references:
Genesis 3:5-6; Hebrews 5:13-14; Ephesians 4:15; James 1:5; Romans 12:1; John 4:31-34; Hebrews 5:13; Mark 4:13; Philippians 4:19

Discussion questions:

1. Based on this review of Adam and Eve, with what choice were they presented? Did this seem like it was a crucial choice? Are we presented with similar choices daily? Explain your answer.

2. What is the difference between earthly wisdom and God's wisdom? Give some examples.

3. Based on what we just read, how does good versus evil compare to single- vs double-minded?

4. We tend to think of babies as innocent and mature people as being wise. Discuss the concepts of innocent, wise, infants, and mature within the context of good versus evil and single-minded versus double-minded.

5. How do we become mature and wise in God? How do this maturity and wisdom compare to the world's version?

Author's favorite quote:

"God knew what was best for them. He wanted them to stay innocent. To not have to decide. To not have to debate. To not have to suffer. He didn't want them to have to discern the difference between good and evil. Put simply, God didn't want Adam and Eve to have to deal with double-mindedness by eating the tree. Living single-minded was His original design."

Session take-away:

Our Heavenly Father truly does know what is best for us, and yet, like Adam and Eve, we often do not grasp the importance and necessity of following Father's instructions. We look at His instructions much like Eve did and allow other voices to speak their brand of wisdom into our ears. We then begin to negotiate with God and make the decision to go our own way instead of the way Father has instructed. How do you negotiate with God-given instructions? Where do you eat from the tree? What else have you gained from this session?

____
____
____
____

PRAYER:

Father,

You know best! I choose to follow Your instructions and not debate or second guess what You say. I choose to stay in the good, in single-minded trust, and not fall into evil double-minded thinking. Show me Your way and I will obey You.

In Jesus' name,
Amen.

Session 11

This session is a continuation of our exploration of "good vs evil." We are learning that "good" pertains to staying single-minded concerning Father's instructions, and "evil" is anything that deviates from those instructions. We discovered that when Adam and Eve listened to a voice other than God's, they entered into the realm of double-minded thinking and living. We will continue to study this concept, how this relates to maturity, and how Jesus modeled this for us as we finish chapter 4 in *Modeling Jesus: Walking Singleminded in a Doubleminded World.*

Presession questions:

1. What caused the struggle that Adam and Eve had with the instructions of Father? In what ways do you find that you have a similar struggle?

2. What is wisdom? How does one gain wisdom? How does James 1:5-8 apply to this discussion?

3. How does the world define maturity? How does this differ from a biblical understanding of maturity? Which definition do you feel fits you best and why?

Read: Good vs Evil (ch4) part 2(pg 34-39)
(9:19 min)(audio 1:16:09-1:25:28)

Scripture references:

Genesis 3:5-6; Hebrews 5:13-14; Ephesians 4:15; James 1:5; Romans 12:1; John 4:31-34; Hebrews 5:13; Mark 4:13; Philippians 4:19

Discussion questions:

1. Adam and Eve debated the instructions of Father. The author states, "We have all debated in our thinking." How prone are you to debate the instructions of Father? What causes the debate? What areas of your life are you most apt to debate?

2. What do you think are God's priorities? What is the difference between Father's business and your business? How do Matthew 6:33, Romans 8:32, and Romans 12:1-3 pertain to this concept?

3. In John 4, Jesus encounters the woman at the well. Discuss ways that Jesus demonstrates following Father's instruction instead of the ways of man. How might these opportunities to make a choice between man's way and God's way present themselves in your life?

4. Discuss John 4:31-34. How does this compare to Hebrews 5:13-14? Based on this understanding what does your "spiritual diet" consist of the most: milk or meat? Explain.

5. "Singleminded vs doubleminded," "good vs evil," "milk vs meat," how are all these terms connected to the parable of the sower? How did Jesus model them for us?

Author's favorite quote:

"Jesus always models the will of the Father. He always lays His will down for the instructions given to Him by Holy Spirit. He is our example to follow, and, in my opinion, He is the only example to follow."

Session take-away:

Think about this favorite quote from the author. If Jesus did it, that follows the Father, should you? How do we make Kingdom business our business too? What else did you gain from this session and a deepened understanding of "good vs. evil?"

____
____
____
____
____
____
____

Prayer:

Father,

Thank You for Jesus, my example in everything. Help me today to lay down my will for Yours today. Teach me what it means to be about Your business instead of my own business. Let me see what Your priorities are today and make them my own.

In Jesus' name,
Amen.

Session 12

Jesus models for us. He is our example in everything. If we look at the way He followed Father's instructions no matter what it was, we can gain valuable insight into the way that we can "walk single-minded in a double-minded world." In this session, we will explore Jesus' example of following Father's instructions even when the going was rough and the outcome in the natural could be perceived as failure.

Presession questions:

1. What is the difference between being "outcome-based" and "obedience-based?"

2. Have you ever tried to follow Father's instructions and had the outcome seem to be a failure? What were the instructions and why did it seem a failure? How do preconceived ideas and personal expectations make outcomes seem more important than obedience?

3. Remember back to the "heroes of faith," did the instructions to Abraham "make sense?" What about Noah, the children of Israel in the wilderness, or at Jericho? When God gives you instructions but not details, how do you handle being obedient?

Read: Jesus Models For Us (ch5) (pg 40-45)
(10:05 min)(audio 1:25:28-1:35:33)

Scripture references:
Mark 4:35-41; Luke 8:22-25; Genesis 3:6; James 1:2-4; Mark 4:36-37; John 4:40; 1 John 4:17; Deuteronomy 31:6; Hebrews 13:5

Discussion questions:

1. Compare and contrast faith vs. knowledge and faith vs. feeling. How do you shut your mind down and "trust" God?

2. Do you think Jesus always understood why Father's instructions were what they were? Was He able to sleep in the back of the boat because He was Jesus or because He trusted His Father completely? If He is our example in everything, then how does this apply to us? How does 1 John 4:17 apply here?

3. The disciples, who were experienced fishermen, were not sufficient for this situation. They knew the waters, they understood storms, but their understanding wasn't enough. Their "I know" how to get this done was not enough to carry them through. Have you experienced any storms in your life that your understanding was not enough to get you through? How did you get through it?

____
____
____
____
____
____
____

4. Look again at James 1:5-8 in the Message Bible. What does it mean to "worry their prayers?" How does this compare to being double-minded? What perspective do we pray from, one of needing answers or one of needing the One Who has the answers?

____
____
____
____
____
____
____

5. If we are about Father's business and we encounter difficulties, are those difficulties like the waves? Are they stirred up by a storm that the enemy is stirring up to get us off track? Think about a time in your life where you thought that you had instructions from Father. Was it clear sailing to carry out those instructions or was your journey challenged?

____
____
____
____
____
____
____

Author's favorite quote:

"Often, we want to figure out what God is doing. Sometimes we even put our spin on it. But if we know exactly how to do it, wouldn't we be seeing from our own knowledge?"

Session take-away:

Discuss the author's favorite quote. What does it mean to "put our spin" on what Father is doing? How do we go to the "other side?" How do we stop questioning Father at every point? What else did you gain from this session?

____

____

____

____

____

____

____

Prayer:

Father,

I confess that I do not always understand what You are doing. My "I knows" often gets in the way. Sometimes I think I understand when I don't and I put my own spin on things instead of checking in with You and learning to see things from Your perspective. Help me to trust you in everything and not go by what I think or feel. Help me to follow Your instructions whether they make sense to me or not. Help me to continue to obey You even when it seems that the outcome of Your instructions is not what I want it to be. Teach me to truly be single-minded to You.

In Jesus' name,
Amen.

Session 13

This session explores the concept of single- and double-mindedness as found in the account of Jonah. The first of two sessions from Jonah chapter 6 in "Modeling Jesus: Walking Singleminded in a Doubleminded World." While many have heard the story of Jonah as a child's Bible story, there is so much that one can learn about following the instructions of Father. It is possible to hear clearly what Father wants and yet determine not to do what He wants in one's own thinking. Jonah is a clear example of one who listened, didn't like what He heard, decided to go his way, and yet in the end, God's will prevailed.

Presession questions:

1. Have you ever had instructions from Father that didn't make sense or, worse yet, put you in a position to do something that you didn't want to do? What did He ask you to do? Did you do it? What was the outcome?

____

____

____

____

____

____

____

2. Based on our last session, do you think Jesus always understood Father's instructions? Do you think Jesus always wanted to do His Father's instruction?

____

____

____

____

____

____

____

3. Do Father's instructions ever challenge our thoughts or prejudices concerning other people that are different from us? How do our culture, family, race, gender, or preconceived ideas get in the way of our walking single-mindedly?

____

____

____

Read: Jonah (Part 1) (pg 46-51)
(10:15min)(audio 1:35:36-1:45:51)

Scripture references:
Jonah; 1 Samuel 15:22; Mark 4; 2 Corinthians 5:7; Luke 22:42; Matthew 12:40; 1 John 4:17

Discussion questions:

1. Jonah knew God was faithful to His word. Jonah knew that since God was telling Him to preach in Nineveh, God planned to save the Ninevites. Due to Jonah's hatred of the Ninevites, he made a choice to disobey God and go his own way. Have there been times in your life when God's instructions have placed you in a position of ministering to someone with whom you have been in opposition? Did you try to "run from the presence of God" like Jonah? How did that work for you?

2. Have you ever encountered a storm in your life that you know is a storm of your making? Were you able to sleep in that storm like Jonah? How did you get out of it?

3. How have your storms of disobedience affected others around you? Have others suffered as a consequence of your actions? How do you correct this?

4. Are there currently any areas of your life where you need to go back to the last thing Holy Spirit said to you and ask for clarification? Even amid Jonah's disobedience, God had prepared a way of rescue for Jonah. Are the circumstances you are in right now the storm or the rescue from your disobedience? Is it possible to know the difference?

AUTHOR'S FAVORITE QUOTE:

"Obviously, Jonah didn't want to do as God told him. He had no care or concern for Nineveh. The reality is that the Hebrews hated the Ninevites. Jonah was no different, and he chose to become double-minded to God's instructions."

SESSION TAKE-AWAY:

How am I double-minded to God's instructions for my life?Why do many choose to go their way and disregard Holy Spirit? What else can you take away from this session?

Prayer:

Father,

Please remove from me any prejudice or preconceived ideas about others that would prevent me from being able to be single-minded about Your business to "seek and save that which is lost." Find any lost places in me so that what You want would be my top priority no matter what You instruct me to do.

In Jesus' name,
Amen.

Session 14

This session will finish chapter 6 on Jonah, comparing Jesus's time on the water in the storm and Jonah's encounter. Here we will see how the experience of storms encountered during single-minded obedience differs from the experience of those storms created due to our double-minded disobedience.

Presession questions:

1. Have you ever had instructions from Father to follow which you initially did not obey, only to find yourself faced with those instructions later on down the road of your life? What happened?

2. How can we tell the difference between a storm of resistance and a storm of disobedience?

3. Why didn't Jonah want to obey God? Is it possible that we miss what God wants to do because we don't have His heart/mind for certain people/ situations? Are we more about ourselves and what we want than we are about what Father wants?

Read: Jonah (Part 2) (pg 51-56)
(11:19 min)(audio1:45:51-1:57:10)

Scripture references:
Jonah; 1 Samuel 15:22; Mark 4; 2 Corinthians 5:7; Luke 22:42; Matthew 12:40; 1 John 4:17

Discussion questions:

1. Distraught sailors awakened Jonah. Distraught disciples awakened Jesus. Whether the storm was from the enemy or disobedience, others were impacted by the storm. How have your life storms impacted others in your life? Which type of storm, enemy, or disobedience? How was the storm quieted?

2. Compare and contrast the initial "outcome" of Jonah's mission in Nineveh with Jesus' mission in the Gadarenes. Which man appeared to have the greater outcome? Does this seem "fair" when Jonah had been disobedient? Are what we perceive as outcomes the true measure, or does the outcome belong to the Lord, and our job is only to stay single-minded to what He asks us to do?

3. When are we equipped to handle problems/storms in our lives? How can we keep the right perspective concerning Father's business versus our business? What should we do when we don't like Father's business and would rather be about our own business?

4. How does catching God's heart and desire change us? How does knowing God on an intimate level affect the way we deal with our life situations?

Author's favorite quote:

"God asked him again if he would go to Nineveh and tell the city to repent. This time Jonah had enough sense to obey, and God gave him another chance."

Session take-away:

Looking at the author's quote Jonah obeyed God the second time around. God is the God of second, third, and each new chance. How do we learn to quickly repent for our double-mindedness? How do we become someone Father can depend on? What else have you gleaned from this session?

Prayer:

Father,

Thank You that You are the God of the second chance and more. Thank You that You allow me to make course corrections if I will repent and turn toward You. Please help me to see things through Your eyes and not just my own. Give me Your perspective and give me Your heart. Help me to stay clear of storms of disobedience by doing what You instruct the first time. Help me to handle the storms of resistance in my life the way that Jesus did, understanding my authority as I am staying in obedience to Your instructions.

In Jesus' name,
Amen.

Session 15

This session looks at Jehoshaphat as an example of both single-minded- and double-mindedness. As we saw in our sessions on Jonah, Jehoshaphat's focus affected himself and others. In Jonah's case, his double-mindedness affected the mariners and, had he not finally obeyed, could have adversely affected the Ninevites. Here, with Jehoshaphat, we see that he had a Godly effect on Judah in his single-mindedness. However, in his double-mindedness, he put himself and his nation in peril.

Presession questions:

1. How is it possible that we can be both single-minded and double-minded concerning the things of God? What things influence our perspective and place double-mindedness as an option for our consideration?

2. How do preconceived ideas, prejudice, and previous experiences lead to our holding onto double-minded thinking even when it is clearly contrary to the teaching of scripture? Why do you think "God said it!" is not always a strong enough reason for our walking in single-mindedness?

3. How can friends, family, and other alliances convince us to hold a double-minded position? Discuss areas that the influence of others causes a genuine internal struggle within you.

Read: Jehoshaphat (pg 57-62)
(11:01min)(audio 1:57:10-2:08:11)

Scripture references:
2 Chronicles 17-21; John 4:24; Proverbs 16:7

Discussion questions:

1. Jehosophat became tempted to double-mindedness and to go his own way. This occurred when others distracted him from his original assignment from God. This can happen to us as well. How do we overcome this type of temptation?

2. When we read of Ahab's scheme of dressing Jehoshaphat in his robe and putting him in his chariot, it seems almost comical that Jehoshaphat would go along with this idea. Have you ever been talked into doing something contrary to what God has told you to do? When you look back on it, what kind of scheme were you talked into?

3. What does it appear that Jehoshaphat learned from the near-disaster at Ramoth-Gilead? How did Jehoshaphat respond differently as recorded in 2 Chronicles 20?

4. Is the key to serving God never making a mistake or always being quick to repent? How does the spirit of religion try to trap us in our mistakes? Refer back to session 1 for the discussion of the spirit of religion.

5. How does worship help us to stay single-minded in the midst of a battle? What happens when we fellowship with fear, doubt, and anger? How does worship combat the enemy?

Author's favorite quote:

"To model Jesus, we can never consider the Father's word an option. God, who is not double-minded, is the safest place for us to abide. Always, without question."

Session take-away:

Consider the author's favorite quote. Obeying God is our place of safety. When Jehosophat decided to follow God and become single-minded, Father always blessed him. How do we get to that point in our lives as well? The place where we no longer deviate? What else are you taking away from this session?

____
____
____
____
____
____
____

Prayer:

Father,

You are my place of safety. I stay in that place by obeying You. Help me follow your instructions no matter what others may say to me to persuade me otherwise. Help me make no unholy alliances. When I do miss the mark, I ask that You give me a spirit of repentance and draw me deeper into fellowship with You. I choose not to fellowship with fear, doubt, anger, depression, or any other entity that tries to vie for my attention or distract me from Your instructions. I choose to stand against the spirit of religion. I do not accept its gifts. I choose You. I do not consider Your instructions optional. I choose to worship You during every battle. You are my only plan.

In Jesus' name,
Amen.

Session 16

This session will discuss the concept of being single-minded related to staying focused on what God has told you and not allowing distractions to deter you from accomplishing that which God has spoken to you.

Presession questions:

1. How does staying focused help you to attain a goal? Discuss a time in your life when you had a specific goal (lose weight, get a particular job, learn something new, etc.). Did you attain it? What did you have to do to arrive at that goal?

____
____
____
____
____
____
____

2. Have you ever experienced a blurry or double vision in your natural eyesight? How did that condition affect the way you walked and "did life?" Was it difficult to go forward with your daily activities?

____
____
____
____
____
____
____

3. Have you ever tried to navigate through a dark room? Did you step on the kids' legos, trip over something on the floor, or kick the bedpost with your little toe? What was that experience like? What happened? Discuss the experience.

____
____
____
____
____

Read: If Your Eye Be Single (pg 63-68)
(11:41 min) (audio 2:08:13-2:19:54)

Scripture reference:
Matthew 6:22; James 1:8; 1 John 2:9; John 16:13; James 1:2-8; Isaiah 53; John 12; Joshua 24:14; Romans 12:1; John 1:5-7; Psalm 119:105; Jeremiah 29:11

Discussion questions:

1. Based on tonight's reading, how should you set goals? What would be the result of learning to focus on Father's instructions? Does this apply only to spiritual goals? Is there any difference for you between spiritual and earthly goals? Should there be? How does Jeremiah 29:11, John 16:13, Isaiah 53:1, Joshua 24:14, and John 12:42-43 apply to goals?

2. Discuss single-minded focus vs. double-minded focus. From presession question number two, apply the experiences in natural activities to how our single vs. double focus affects our ability to walk with God and be about His business. What would the difference between blurry vision and double-vision be in this context? How do we overcome blurry vision? How do we overcome double-vision? How does James 1:8 apply to this discussion?

3. Think back on our experiences walking in the dark, and compare them to walking in the dark spiritually. How do 1 John 1:5-7 and 1 John 2:9 help us understand "walking in the light?" What does Psalm 119:15 tell us will aid us in walking in the light?

4. What is the difference between acting and reacting? How does our choice to stay single-minded affect our ability to act instead of reacting? How does acting compare to "being in the light" and rcacting compare to "being in the dark?" How does God bring life and light into our situations?

AUTHOR'S FAVORITE QUOTE:

"The word *single*, used here, is speaking of being focused and deliberately working toward attaining a specific end (or goal or outcome). This verse states that the result of this single-minded determination to the Word of God is that now your body will be full of light. Light is the life of God. It is good to have light and life flowing through us."

SESSION TAKE-AWAY:

Looking at the author's favorite quote from this session, when have you truly noticed and felt His light and life flowing through you? Tell of an experience? What would living in “that place” full time, the place of light and life, be like on a continual, daily basis? What are you taking away from this session?

____
____
____
____

Prayer:

Father,

Cause my vision to be single. Cause my focus to be sharp. Help me to have single-minded determination to follow Your word so I will walk in the light and not in darkness. I receive Your light into my being, and I thank You that Your light dispels all darkness.

In Jesus' name,
Amen

Session 17

Pastor Brad has often said, "If anyone ever advertised a 'Patience' conference, it would probably not be well attended." In this session, the topic of patience will be discussed and how it is a crucial component in the process of learning to "walk single-minded in a double-minded world."

Presession questions:

1. How do you define patience? Do you consider yourself a patient person? What is the evidence of patience in your life?

2. What is your attitude like when you encounter difficulties, problems, and storms in your life? What do you do when you don't know what to do?

3. Define peace. What do you think is the connection between peace and patience?

Read: Patience (pg 69-76)
(16:36 min) (audio 2:20:00-2:36:24)

Scripture references:
James 1:2; Hebrews 12:2; James 1:3-4; John 11:9; James 1:5-6; Hebrews 11:6; Mark 4; James 1:7; Romans 14:23; James 1:8; Isaiah 26:3

Discussion questions:

1. Compare James 1:4 and Hebrews 5:14. What is the relationship between patience and maturity? How does this relate to good vs. evil? What does being patient show about your ability to be single-minded?

2. What are miracles? How would walking single-minded possibly affect the need for miracles? Is there a place in God where miracles are a lifestyle instead of an event?

3. Was Peter operating in patience? How might things have been different if he had? Rewrite a possibility for Peter's walk on the water, based on a patient Peter instead of a distracted one. How do distractions push your ability to be patient?

4. Running in the sand is harder than running on hard ground. Pastor Brad often says, "Don't waste the sand," and "never waste a problem." How does this apply to building endurance? How is patience related to endurance?

Author's favorite quote:

"The King James translation interprets patience as endurance. But look at the single-minded veracity of the writer. He is telling us to be joyful when we enter into a trial or problem, speaking to us as if we know something. Insider information, if you will. Our faith can be measured by how patient we are. Strong faith can be measured by the level of patience and calm we operate in."

Session take-away:

Why does the world/church, as usual, struggle with patience? Do they not understand it? What are you taking away from this session on patience?

Prayer:

Father,

Thank You for your patience. Thank you that I can run in the sands of life and build up my spiritual muscles. Thank you that I don't ever need to waste a problem, but in each situation, I can draw closer to You and learn that You always have the answer. Thank You that as I grow in patience Your word assures me that I am becoming more mature, more whole and that I will lack for nothing. Help me to have my mind stayed on You, to stay single-minded on who You are and on what You have instructed me.

In Jesus' name,
Amen

Session 18

In this session, Pastor Brad shares with his readers when he discovered the key to seeing people through Father's perspective and how that has changed his life and ministry.

Presession questions:

1. Have you ever felt like you knew something clearly but you just couldn't seem to get anyone else to hear it? What do you think kept you from being able to convey what you knew to others? Was the difficulty in you or them?

2. What do you feel is in a relationship that gives a person a right to speak into your life? How can you tell if someone genuinely cares for you or if you are just a "project" that they are working on?

3. What do you think keeps the church from being more effective in the world today? Is it the responsibility of the church to be "right?" How does the spirit of religion, that was discussed in the first session, work at keeping the church from being "the answer for the word today?"

READ: MY GREAT AWAKENING (pg 77-82)
(10:17 min) (audio 2:36:24-2:46:41)

SCRIPTURE REFERENCES:
Romans 2:4; Romans 12:10; 1 John 4:20

DISCUSSION QUESTIONS:

1. What does it mean for a "Revelation to be wrapped in love?" What difference does this make for the receiver/hearer? What happens when a revelation is released without love? Is this concept only for five-fold ministers? If not, how does it apply to each person?

2. What is the difference between the call to "love My children" and the call to "Come up higher?" Why do you think that Holy Spirit would emphasize the first call and not the second? Why do you think we would emphasize the second?

3. What is ministry? What is the reason for ministry? Who is called to ministry? What is the outworking of that call?

4. What is the connection between "walking single-minded in a double-minded world" and "walking in love?"

____
____
____
____
____
____
____

AUTHOR'S FAVORITE QUOTE:

While teaching in front of a congregation in Canada, I heard myself saying these words: " The reason Holy Spirit would not release the single- and double-minded revelation was because I had not walked in enough love for others at that point in my ministry." This is the only reason the single-minded revelation was in limbo? I thought.

SESSION TAKE-AWAY:

For years Pastor Brad had the important revelation of "walking single-minded," and yet he had been hindered from sharing it effectively because of the condition of his own personal love walk. What is hidden in your life that makes you unable to be used as effectively as the Holy Spirit desires? How do you uncover those areas? What else are you taking away from this session?

____
____
____
____
____
____
____

Prayer:

Father,

Teach me to walk in love with You and others so I can be effective in all that You desire. Help me to be single-minded and unhindered in loving as You love. Give me Your heart.

In Jesus' name,
Amen.

Session 19

What began as a great awakening for Pastor Brad became a deep exploration into what love really is and how a truly single-minded walk must be a walk of love. Even though there may be other components to that single-minded walk that Jesus modeled for us, ultimately, "It All Works By Love." In this session, we will explore how walking in love has become a trigger statement, and although we say it, we fall short of actually doing it.

Presession questions:

1. How do you define love? When you hear the phrase, "walk in love," what does that mean to you?

2. What does it look like to walk in love? Does it mean to be nice to people? Does it mean never to get upset? How do you "walk in love?"

3. Discuss a time when you heard the words "I love you," but the person's actions conveyed a different message than their words. Has your experience in life been one where you sensed you were loved? How or how not?

Read: It All Works By Love (pg 83-87)
(8:10 min)(audio 2:46:43 - 2:54:53)

Scripture references:
John 14:15, 21, 23-24; 1 Peter 1:19-20; Exodus 20:1-17; Matthew 22:36-40; Matthew 24:35; 1 John 4:20-21; James 1:7-8; Matthew 5:43-48

Discussion Questions:

1. Discuss the four words used in Greek: *stergo, phileo, eros,* and *agape,* which are all interpreted in English by the word love. What is the difference between saying you love your spouse, children, dog, pizza, car, or God? When we use the same word love for all of these things, does the true meaning of the concept of love get distorted in our thinking?

____
____
____
____
____
____
____

2. What is the difference between truly "walking in love" and only giving lip service to the concept? Is it only about the way we behave toward others? Or is it possible to behave correctly and yet not truly walk in love? Is it possible to only have a polished performance of correct behavior and still have hatred in your heart? Or is it possible to behave correctly and yet not truly walk in love?

____
____
____
____
____
____
____

3. John was known as the disciple that Jesus loved. Perhaps he had a revelation of how Jesus modeled the "love walk." What do John 14:15, 21, 23-24 tell us about how Jesus says a person demonstrates their "love walk?" Was this what Jesus modeled? How did He model it for us? What was Jesus' single-minded instruction on walking in love? What is the connection between love and obedience?

4. How could our desire to walk our way, in double-mindedness, demonstrate areas of our lives where we need to make corrections? What might some of these areas be?

5. What is the relationship between maturity and your love walk?

Author's favorite quote:

"A mature believer is one who walks in love. A mature believer is one who knows how to be obedient to Heavenly instructions. A mature believer is one who knows how to discern between good and evil. A mature believer is one who lives in the heavenly realm - the realm of fellowshipping and following Father."

Session take-away:

How mature are you based on your "love-walk"? Are you mature because you only treat others with respect? Are you mature because you follow Father and His directives instead? What else have you learned in this session?

____

____

____

____

____

____

____

PRAYER:

Father,

Clarify to me what love really means. Show me how to love You and how to love others. Heal the wounds from the past experiences where someone said they loved me but it was something other than real love. Erase from my mind the world's definition of love and replace it with Your definition. Show me the difference between walking in love and only lip service. Deepen my understanding of how Jesus walked in love in every situation and help me to love the way He does. Show me the areas of my heart where I want to go my own way and help me to turn them over to You.

In Jesus' name,
Amen.

Session 20

In this session, we will continue to explore how walking in love is a crucial characteristic of a mature believer. We will look at how the ten commandments found in Exodus 20 are summed up by Jesus in Matthew 22 and demonstrate that "It All Works By Love." Both our relationship with God and our relationship with others must be a walk of love. Duty to God and duty to man are not enough alone. And there is a third aspect of this love walk that is greatly distorted today. We shall explore this three-fold love walk in greater depth.

Presession questions:

1. What are the ten commandments? Are they just rules to follow? Do you see the ten commandments as applying to life today? Is following the ten commandments legalism? What would it look like to follow them?

2. What do you think the ten commandments have to do with walking in love? Which of the words for love from the last session would you think would be the kind of love that would be appropriate here and why?

3. Which commandments do you think are the most difficult to follow and why? Do you think there is an easier way, to sum up these "rules" for living?

Read: It All Works By Love (pg 88-92)
(11:24 min)(audio 2:54:53 - 3:06:17)

Scripture references:
John 14:15, 21, 23-24; 1 Peter 1:19-20; Exodus 20:1-17; Matthew 22:36-40; Matthew 24:35; 1 John 4:20-21; James 1:7-8; Matthew 5:43-48

Discussion Questions:

1. Discuss what you believe motivated the expert in Jewish law to ask Jesus, "What is the greatest commandment?" Do you think he got the answer he expected? What do you think Jesus' answer revealed about the one asking the question?

2. What is the connection between the ten commandments (Exodus 20:1-17) and walking in love? How did Jesus clarify that in Matthew 22:36-4?

3. Jesus said that we were to love God and love others. How do we demonstrate that we love God? What does it mean to love others as you love yourself? How is the concept of self-love twisted in today's society?

4. Discuss Matthew 5:43-48. Is our love walk just to be with nice people? People, we like? People, that think as we do? What about only "good" people? Moral people? Discuss the tension in learning to see people the way Father sees them. Is it possible to love on this level?

Author's favorite quote:

"Can learning to live in the divine life automatically get us to the place where we truly prefer our brother? It would let us discover Him in His word and scripture. It would teach us to act and operate the way He does."

Session take-away:

Sum up what you have learned in this lesson. Do I act and operate on the Heavenly plain? Am I acting and operating in the love Jesus spoke of?

Prayer:

Father,

Jesus said that the greatest of all Your instructions to us was to love You with everything we are and love others as we love ourselves. I want to love You with all that I am. Teach me how. Give me Your ability to love as You do. Help me to have Your kind of love for everyone, including myself. Give me the desire to prefer my brother above myself. I want to not only hear Your heartbeat but to have mine beat just like Yours.

In Jesus' name,
Amen.

Session 21

In this session, Pastor Brad explores the concept of resolve. He defines resolve as having a strong determination to do something or deciding firmly on a course of action. In the theme of this book, we see that Jesus modeled a strong resolve to hear His Father and follow only His instructions. We will see the importance of resolve for us if we are going to "walk single-minded in a double-minded world."

Presession questions:

1. Have you ever set a goal for yourself that required setting everything else aside to achieve? For example: losing weight, setting a record, writing a book, etc. What did you have to stop/start/continue to do to arrive at your goal? Did you achieve it? Why/why not?

2. Has anyone else ever had an expectation/goal that they set for you? Were you 100% "on board" with their plan? Why/why not? What motivates you to accomplish goals in your daily life?

3. How easily are you talked out of your position? Do you think there is a difference between resolve and willpower? Is this just motivational, or is there a spiritual component?

Read: Resolve (pg 93-100)
(15:01min)(audio 3:06:18 - 3:21:19)

Scripture references:
Hebrews 12:1-4; Hebrews 11; Luke 16:1-10

Discussion Questions:

1. Jesus says that the "children of this world are more shrewd in their generation than the children of light." What does this statement mean to you? What do you think the word shrewd means? Explore how shrewd in both English and the Greek word translated here has the concept of judging a situation and setting the mind on a course of action.

2. If the world can accomplish great goals based on motivation and willpower, shouldn't we see that with Holy Spirit and the instructions of our Father, we can accomplish even greater goals? What are we missing when it comes to resolving to stay single-minded to our Father's instructions?

3. What might happen if we did what the world does, concerning their goals when it comes to having resolve concerning the things of God? Do we lack resolve because we don't believe that Father's instructions apply to us? Are we

not that convinced that Father's instructions are the way to reach our goals, or are our goals not lined up with His goals?

4. Is our relationship with our Father about us? Are we turning to Him to help us meet our goals, or are we going to Him first to find out what goals He has for us in His Business? How resolved are we to partner with our Father and help Him win this world for Jesus? How do we become a part of the Body that our Father can depend on day-to-day?

5. What does it mean to you to resolve to "walk single-minded in a double-minded world?" Give examples of how Jesus modeled resolve for us. What does Hebrews 12:1-3 tell us about Jesus' resolve?

Author's favorite quote:

"Resolve is defined as "deciding firmly on a course of action." Another dictionary defines it this way: "As a noun, resolve refers to a strong determination to do something."

"I believe the church is entering the best time to serve our Father. I believe and see a positive attitude in the church about winning this world. My opinion is that some of the greatest miracles ever to occur are coming upon us. I think real church history will be made in the next few years."

Session take-away:

What course of action have you firmly decided on? Are you strongly determined to find out what Father wants from you and how He sees you as His partner? Are you resolved to be about Father's business and be a history maker in the years ahead? What else have you learned from this session?

____
____
____
____
____
____
____

Prayer:

Father,

Let true spiritual resolve come into my being so I may be single-minded about what You want and accomplish what You have prepared me to do on this earth. I confess that my soulish willpower is not enough to keep me going on the path You have designed for me. But You are my God, and there is no one else worthy of my resolve. You are my highest goal and my greatest prize. Give me Your ability to set my face like flint toward You. Your instructions are my course of action. I will reach the prize.

In Jesus' name,
Amen.

Session 22

This session explores the concept of partnership with God. As we are resolved to follow His instructions in everything, we find that our lives are more than just about living out our days on this earth, doing what we want. We are on this planet for a purpose, God's purpose. He wants us to grow up into the family business and be His partner to "seek and save that which is lost." Jesus stated that this was His purpose on the earth and said that "just as the Father sent me so send I you" (John 20:21).

Presession questions:

1. What is different about being a partner from being an employee? Have you ever been in a partnership? Are the responsibilities different? Are the rewards different? Explain.

2. What qualities would you look for in someone with whom you were going to go into partnership? What qualities do you believe you would bring?

3. Define the following: servant, friend, and son. How do these words relate to being in a partnership?

Read: Partnership -- Being About Our Father's Business (pg 101-107)(13:31 min)(audio 3:21:21 - 3:34:52)

Scripture references:

2 Peter 3:9; Genesis 18:16-33; Hebrews 4:16; Luke 2:41-50, John 5:30-32; Amos 3:3

Discussion questions:

1. Abraham was called a servant and a friend of God. God trusted him. He was someone with whom God chose to "hang out!" Abraham was in partnership with God. Review Genesis 18:16-33. How did Abraham get to this place? Do you see yourself as someone God would choose to trust on this level? How do we get to this place?

2. What is your definition of a friend? Of fellowship? Of awareness? How does the author's explanation of friendship, fellowship, and awareness help you to grow in your understanding of how Father sees you?

3. Jesus' partnership, His awareness, and fellowship with His Father can be seen throughout the Gospels. Discuss further what Luke 2:41-50 and John 5:30-32 reveal about what Jesus modeled. What other verses can you think of that demonstrate this concept?

4. What is a joint venture? What does it mean to partake? How do 2 Peter 3:9, Hebrews 4:16, and Amos 3:3 apply to these concepts?

5. Does it seem that partnership with God is too much to attain? Do you think this is a position of arrogance? Why would Father want to partner with us?

AUTHOR'S FAVORITE QUOTE:

"He wants more of our time, more of our awareness, more of our fellowship, and - I believe strongly - He wants to be able to depend on us to partner with Him and to be about our Father's business."

SESSION TAKE-AWAY:

How much of us does He really have? How do we learn to do His business and not our own? Is there a place where we stop worrying about our needs and become strong enough to partner with Him and do His will? What else did you gain from this session?

Prayer:

Father,

I am amazed that You want to partner with me to seek and save the lost. I confess that You are the Senior Partner and it is Your business. I will choose to follow Your business plan and conduct myself by Your instructions. Help me to see everyone the way that You see them and to treat them the way that You would treat them. Help me to be a partner on whom You can depend. Thank You for this amazing privilege.

In Jesus' name,
Amen.

Session 23

In this session, Pastor Brad sums up the concept of this book with an in-depth exploration of Hebrews 11:6. This is another verse that is pivotal to our understanding of "walking single-minded in a double-minded world."

Presession questions:

1. Discuss your view of how God interacts with you in your life. How aware are you of His presence? How do you interact with Him on a daily basis? How would you describe His leadership in your life?

2. Define the following words: surrender, reward, diligent, and factory recall.

3. Do you think that God would appear and interact with an unbeliever?

Read: A Final Thought (pg 108-118)

(19:41min) (audio 3:34:53 - 3:54:34)

Scripture references:

Hebrews 11:6; Mark 4:13; Mark 5; Matthew 18:3

Discussion questions:

1. Based on the author's comments, how much of a reality is God in your life? Are you only praying, hoping He is out there somewhere listening to you, or do you know that you are sitting down together working things out hand in hand? How real is God's presence to you? How real are His promises to you? When you are "in the grease," in a problem, how stable are you?

____
____
____
____
____
____
____

2. What areas of your life have you surrendered to Him, and what areas do you keep to yourself? How has this changed during this study?

____
____
____
____
____
____
____

3. What do the demoniac of the Gaderenes, the prodigal son, and the woman with the issue of blood all have in common? How do these examples help you understand what you must do to obtain help when you are having difficulties?

____
____
____
____
____
____
____

4. We must believe that God is, and that He is a rewarder. Is it possible to believe that He is and yet not believe that He is a rewarder? In both Hebrew and Greek, the word rewarder means He "pays wages." This is more than just a pat on the back, a trophy, or a medal for doing something well. The fulfillment of His promises are the wages He pays! Is it possible to embrace some of His promises but not all of them? Would you refuse benefits at a job? What are some reasons why we might not receive all that our Father has for us?

5. What does it mean to spend time with God for you, spend time for others, spend time to be, spend time for Him? How are these four different things, and what might we do differently for each?

Author's favorite quote:

"We serve a God who operates only by faith. He does not consider any other way. When we don't use faith, we are in a place of double-mindedness to His will. It is difficult to get an answer to our problems when we don't follow His instructions. Real faith comes by following Him fully. Another word we can use is surrender."

Session take-away:

What areas of my life do I surrender to Him, and what areas do I keep to myself? How do I stay in faith and keep my focus on His instructions and do the task at hand?

____

____

____

____

Prayer:

Father,

Show me what areas I need to surrender to You. I believe that You are and that You are my Rewarder. Help me to always come to You both when things are good and when I am in need. I want to learn to be a mature faith being just like You.

Amen.

Session 24

In this final session, we will review the main points covered in this book and discuss what we have learned as we have explored the journey of "**Modeling Jesus: Walking Single-minded in a Double-minded World.**"

Presession questions:

1. How "real" is God to you right now? How has this been affected by this study?

2. How do you spend time with God? How much time do you spend with Him? Does this seem like an academic pursuit, or are you developing a relationship with Him?

3. What are some ways that we can learn to hear Him? Does He speak to everyone the same way? Do you believe you hear Him?

Read: Afterword (pg 119-121)
(5:47 min) (audio 3:54:35 - 4:00:22)

Scripture references:
Matthew 13:46; Ephesians 6:13; Ecclesiastes 12:13

Discussion questions:

1. What is the pearl of great price? How much do you treasure the instructions of your Father? What might it mean to you to "sell all you have?" Are you willing to "sell all you have" to be single-minded to what He says?

2. From what you have learned from this study, what does it mean to be single-minded? How do we cease being double-minded? Is it this simple? Is this easy? What is the difference between simple and easy?

3. Thinking back on our study, how does winning and losing keep us trapped in double-minded thinking? How then are we to look at situations that seem like failures or successes? If the outcome is not how we judge a situation, what is the measure?

4. What does it mean to "rest" in Him? How do we enter into His rest? Are we able to lie down in the back of the boat with Jesus in the midst of the storm? What must we believe so that we are able to rest?

5. Write your personal testimony of how this study has impacted you.

Author's favorite quote:

“1 - Realize God is real.
2 - Now, get to know Him.
3 - Hear God. (Talk with Him.)
4 - Become single-minded to what He tells you.
5 - Stop being double-minded and second-guessing.
6 - Stop looking at winning and losing. (How things look in the natural, worldly realm.)
7 - Rest. Rest in what you heard. Rest in what He is doing."

Session take-away:

How has your understanding of the concept of single-minded vs. double-minded changed throughout this study? How has the parable found in Mark 4 helped you see yourself and the challenges you have to walk as Jesus modeled for us? How do I learn to follow the seven steps listed above? How do we make them a reality in our lives?

____

____

____

____

PRAYER:

Father,

Thank You for the reality of who You are. I want to know You. Help me to know You more every day. Teach me to listen to You. I am Yours, and I can hear You. Help me to grow more single-minded every day. To put Your instructions, Your voice, Your leading as my only focus. I choose to stop second-guessing and being double-minded. I choose Your report over all others. I choose to stop looking at how things seem in this natural realm, and I choose to see everything from Your perspective and vantage point. You know best, and I rest in what You say. I rest in what You are doing. I choose to lie down in the back of the boat in the midst of the storm because I single-mindedly obey You when You tell me to go to the other side in any situation. Thank You for being my single-minded example!

In Jesus' name,
Amen.

Conclusion

Thank you for participating in this study……

Made in the USA
Middletown, DE
28 January 2022